RANDALL the Blue Spider
Plays Pretend

Written by
Ryeson & Shana Bull

Illustrated by
Brady Lovell

EAST 26TH
PUBLISHING

Randall the Blue Spider Plays Pretend
Copyright © 2021 by Shana Bull

All rights reserved. No part of this publication may be reproduced, distributed, or transmitted in any form or by any means, including photocopying, recording, or other electronic or mechanical methods, without the prior written permission of the author and publisher, except in the case of brief quotations embodied in critical reviews and certain other noncommercial uses permitted by copyright law. For permissions requests, contact the publisher at www.east26thpublishing.com

Library of Congress Cataloging-in-Publication data is available
ISBN: (Paperback) 978-1-955077-47-7 | (Hardback) 978-1-955077-46-0 | (eBook) 978-1-955077-48-4

10 9 8 7 6 5 4 3 2 1
First printing edition 2021

East 26th Publishing
Houston, TX

www.east26thpublishing.com

Sometimes they pretend that the playground at their school is a pirate ship.

Other times, they make believe that they live in an underwater world full of giant octopuses and lots of jellyfish.

Today, Randall and Joey found out that their school is hosting a play.

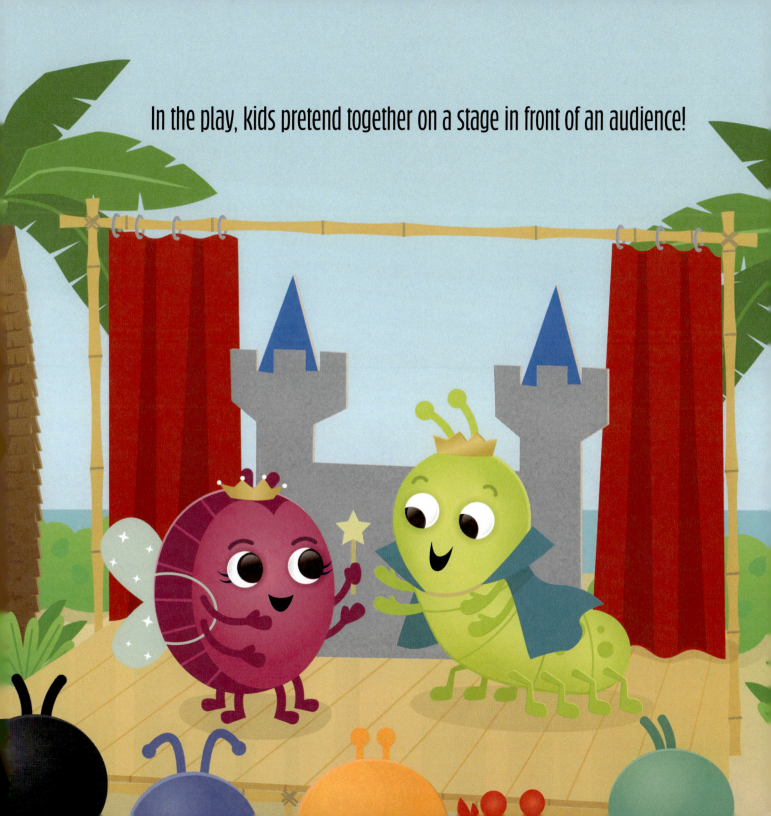

Randall is excited to try out for the play, but Joey is worried.

A stutter means that he sometimes repeats words or sounds when he talks.

One classmate tells Joey he shouldn't try out for the play because of his stutter. Joey feels sad and embarrassed.

Joey tells Randall that he doesn't want to sign up for the play because he doesn't want the bully to keep making fun of him.

Randall knows that kids only bully others because they don't feel good about themselves on the inside.

Using advice his mom gave him, Randall suggests
Joey practice standing up to the bully by acting out what to say first.

After acting it out with Randall, Joey approaches the bully and says, "P-Please--please don't make--don't make fun of my stutter. There is nothing wrong with me. I am great just the way I am. And so are you!"

The bully walks away.

Joey feels proud of himself and the way he handled the situation.

Randall and Joey sign up for the play together and pretend on the stage with their friends.

Soon, Joey discovers that the more times he plays pretend in front of an audience, the less he thinks about his stutter, even if it doesn't go away.

In the next play, Joey is the lead pirate. He stutters a few times but is thrilled when everyone claps for him at the end.

Even the bully who made fun of him.
Now he wants to pretend in a play also!

THE END

DON'T MISS THE OTHER BOOKS IN THIS BESTSELLING SERIES!

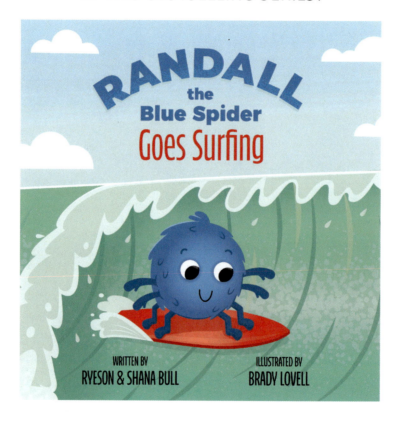

#1 BESTSELLING AUTHORS RYESON & SHANA

By the time baby Ryeson Bull was smiling, he was telling stories with his actions. By age two he memorized *Goodnight Moon* and could repeat every line (yelling, of course). At age two-and-a-half, he dictated the first *Randall the Blue Spider* book to his mama (co-author Shana Bull) in a hospital parking lot in downtown Long Beach.

Ryeson was born with Cystic Fibrosis, a hereditary disease that impacts his lungs and digestive system. The ocean has always been a special place for the Bull family because salt air is good for Ryeson's lungs. Aside from the ocean, Rye loves reading, hiking, and playing outside with friends and random sticks he finds on the ground.

Shana Bull is a freelance writer and digital marketer with a focus on writing about travel, food, wine, music, and family life. Shana loves elaborate cheese boards, rosé wine, and adventures with her husband + Ryeson.

DISCOVER RANDALL & HIS FRIENDS
@randallthebluespider
randallthebluespider.com

Made in the USA
Middletown, DE
11 November 2021